GW01395935

FREEDOM DIALOGUE (II)

The author, who writes for a hobby, is a mathematics teacher and has produced yet another book of pensive poetry — his fifth. As in his first published book Streams, *the thoughtful relaxing prose which stimulates our mind, is once again present in this new volume.*

.

By the same author:

FREEDOM DIALOGUE (II)

J. F. Her

J. F. Her
Nov. 2005

ARTHUR H. STOCKWELL LTD.
Elms Court Ilfracombe Devon
Established 1898

British Library Cataloguing-in-Publication Data.
A catalogue record for this book is available
from the British Library.

ISBN 0 7223 3160-6

Printed in Great Britain by
Arthur H. Stockwell Ltd.
Elms Court   Ilfracombe
Devon

To
Liane Albrecht
Gerard Maher
Conor Maher

CONTENTS

Truth & truth

Truth spoken
May fade into memory
But will echo again
And again

Until
The Origin
Reveals Itself
In the end.

Canto VI (2)

A: The extent of human love is doggish,
With occasional exceptions attaining
A kind of canine-like loyalty.

Human beings, it would appear,
Are dictated to by those regions
Below the neck;

We have ourselves convinced that
We are capable of thought
Where, in actual fact,

Budged we haven't beyond association.
As we approach another cycle's end
Originality runs out:

Like the dog, bedraggled,
Having done his service round —
Spent —

Turns back
And following that rambling track,
Noseys his trail homeward.

P: Behaving like powerful adhesive,
Loyalty bonds true friend to friend

And honourable souls
To truths infinitely greater
Despite the sacrifice;
For the sake of churlish Ingratitude.

Loyalty has lots to do with Love —
As has fidelity:
If everyone served himself alone,
How long would human society endure?

Canto VI (2)

This marks the spot where
Societies go under
That don't atone
For their extremes and excesses — overgrown.

Western society bears witness to self
In sermons on total independence
Whose leitmotives embrace
Other-World sponsored ego-trips.

This drunken Zeitgeist
Drives head-on against
Flow of the human spirit.

People are not geneered
Independent of their fellows.

Bulging at a node, mankind awaits
Prompting . . .
To further evolution.
A: Society is a club of clubs
And like with all clubs,
One must belong, hold membership,
Before one can freely circulate.

Society is no less than
An acceptable form of prostitution:
Loyalty is instinctive,
As is human love, and for that matter
All human behaviour.
The whole ritual of love is but
A residual propensity toward
Primal modes of play.
(pause)
Sex is habit, routine,
An act of unadulterated pleasure,

Canto VI (2)

A power display
Caused by a ravenous impulse
That drives our being.
Boredom or stress — either extreme —
Accelerates this cell machine.
(pause)
Where men and women are most adept
Is in the field of mutual exploitation.
Love, undressed and stripped of make-up:
Symbiosis of self-interest
Says it candid' —
Spits it out!

P: In the procreative urge
One hears none other than
Call of the coming generation.
Pleasure's a factor of natural subvention.

A: *(interjects)*
Must be oversubscribed!

P: *(continues)*
The timeless soul already knows
Each outcome of choice infinite.
There's knowledge so in human stows
Where veiled Futurity may be brought to light.

Libido, cell division on the go,
May be channelled so or so.
(pointing to his head and then to his lower body)

Attraction — magnetic, chemical, etc. —
Draws two entities together
But, singlehandedly,
Love holds the two in place.

So strong a bond is Love
Its grip tends to fusion.

Canto VI (2)

(pause)
Love, a lifetime affair,
Takes no part in revokable arrangements.

Love, a billow,
Has to have an outflow.

Exits off Love's dual-carriageway
Lead into one-way streets.

Anti-love cuts off one traffic lane;
Deadends in self-obsession.

To Love is to be free;
Free of the four prison walls:
Greed, rancour, ignorance, pride.

To have chosen Love,
Opened oneself to Above,
Denotes arrival at maturity;
To have turned one's back on instinct.

A: Loving has to do with business,
Defence of one's own interests,
Survival, social fitness —
Predatory instincts.

P: To its Source alone
True human love clings,
Maintaining detachment
From created things.

A: Pure animal urge
Pushes the human
Over its rational verge.
Woman becomes man's scourge.

P: *(interjects)*
In that case, he must be her penance.

Canto VI (2)

A: *(continues)*
    As far as human relations go
    Detachment has been achieved:

    The nuptial ring was believed to show
    Belonging together of a pair
    As the snow-white bridal gown was
    A statement of no previous affair
    But belonging, in contemporary reality, has
    The speed and substance of modern underwear.

P: An interesting correspondence, admittedly:
    Were it generally true,
    It could be equated derivatively:
    Let's say, $db/ds = u$!

A: *(continues)*
    Belongings — land, livestock, slaves, wives —
    Have always had to do with price;
    Love too takes its economic slice.

P: A person's approach to responsibility
    Plumbs fairly accurately
    The said's maturity.

    Private property Time has shown by far the most
    Expensive illusion a human being can host;
    The body itself we've got not without cost.

A: Property is in no way illusory;
    Private, though, was quietly laid to rest
    Shortly after the discovery:
    Itself within the realm of public interest.

P: When one has loved because . . . ,
    Then clear it is
    The genre of love it was.

    A love that takes, takes
    Or takes for granted

Canto VI (2)

Liaises only with self.
A: The destination we choose
   Determines the road we use.
P: Love breaks the letter of The Law,
   Working seven days a week;
   But nonetheless truly keeps
   Spirit with Father and Son.

. . . Stopping not at reason,
   Love climbs to its highest human height
   To faith;

   Marching on ahead
   Love leads
   Along a narrow mountain track
   To freedom from self —
   Subtlest of slaveries;

   Toward its Cause
   Love disposes
   Naturally arranging, and disciplining its troop;

   Weeding out untruth, injustice, privilege;
   Promoting equality, justice, Truth,
   Love creates and safeguards the conditions for life;

   Tired, Love doesn't know:
   Surging onward,
   While welling upward
   Brimming over and out to overflow

   Freeing captive, slave
   Relieving parched, famished
   Tending sick
   Healing wounded humanity;

Canto VI (2)

Spanning infinity,
Dimensions natural,
And supernatural . . .

A: Your love is a legendary peak
But fabled mountains are impossible to reach.

Why must ideals always be
So elevated, so far afield?
Would not modesty be more laudable?
The more tangible, the more attainable!
P: And inertia
More sustainable!

Love may become as real
Or as ideal
As a person's will allows.

Not taking too kindly to bare rock,
Love languishes:
But on spying a handful of topsoil,
Spurts into life.

Those unprepared to toil,
To stoop, cultivate clay,
Realise weeds, not dreams —
Nature willing, perhaps an odd wild floweret —
Hence 'ideal'!

Those who talk ideals
Are those who cheat and steal
That which they're unwilling
Or unable to earn squarely
And throw a scrap excuse
At growling conscience qualms.

Canto VI (2)

Ideals remain ideal
For habits of state
Averse to change.
Lauded love, that common type,
Can't even claim compromise:
It's Compromise's compromise;
Were it further watered down,
It would dilute water.

Measured compromise has unmeasurable worth
When applied to quench the flames of strife:
But, commissioned as the way of life,
Compromise will grief engulf the earth.
(pause)
Too many love to fairytale —
Reverie, lounge in head;
Then when it comes to Love,
Expect to be spoon-fed.

To put distance between oneself
And want or ignorance
Requires enormous effort:
If someone wants a home,
An education, to repay a loan,
Work, career, one's name in stone,
It's reasonable to accept
That none too advanced concept:
Effort.

So why should Love,
Something worth striving for,
Be sought for second-hand?
Be valued at half-nothing?
A: That's not the way things work,
Not for the most part of the earth.
Without a good head-start,

Canto VI (2)

One's got a fish-out-of-water's odds.

Love, for youth or comfort,
Unburdened with the hand-to-mouth,
Is nice to fantasize about
But after the first attempt at lovey-dove,
No-one further believes in love —
Tis just another Santa Clause.

With men and women
Love is fine
But security rarely needs reminding
To sign on the dotted line.
And, no sooner has the belly been put to bed,
Than carnal consciousness awakens to be fed.

Some years on,
Running from the boredom of
Sex and security,
Couples look for love and comfort
In infidelity.

On Kaiser Str. one pays before;
Lib-love solicits door to door;
Loose-love makes do anywhere;

Bourgeois love, that common bore,
One pays for later,
But must pays more.
P: For those whose loyalties lie that bit nether,
Thoughts of abstinence must be quite sore.

Too much thought spent on oneself
Can only kindle discontent.
Thinking of others raises the mind
To heightier orbits by far

Canto VI (2)

Than thinking of self
Just as loving someone else
Betrays a loftier state of consciousness
Than being loved.

Love resembles the process of the sun:
Two loves collide and greater love is born
Which knows no limit up or down,
Radiating beyond beyond.
(pause)
Within that cognizance, being truly loved,
Nestles the surest security on earth.
Conditional love espouses, not Love,
But a social institution.

A: *(interjects)*
A neat euphemism . . . ,
Not forgetting,
Dealing must double!

P: *(continues)*
A child cuddles into sleep
Indifferent to the world
Peacefully certain within love:
Secure in maternal arms.

Love satisfies itself with enough,
Doing without in preference to
Craving for what it hasn't got.

Adult love's made up of complex stuff:
Riddled through with ifs and buts.

A: There you go again
With that highfalutin guff!
You're trying to attribute
A smooth integument
To a bristly carapace rough!

Canto VI (2)

Open your eyes!
No-one swallows any more
That kind of fluff.

Christian pups we surely are —
Offspring of Christian bitches!

Most of us are by-products
Of female insecurity
And male lust
Or unavoidables just.

Tis an ongoing tragedy,
Not mentioning stark human reality,
In matters of hims and hers
Your love's a poor adhesive.
P: Where pairs share pleasure only —
Otherwise from each other flee —
Or are held together through psychology,
There, logically, Love remains theory.

Since Ideal's being declared unreal,
It can't obtain a landing permit,
Not even on appeal.

But ideals do oversee humankind
And call fallen man
To nobler deeds.

Selfishness does violence
Not only to neighbour
But also to self.

Love, antithesis to Selfishness,
Alone among all activities
Harms nobody.

Canto VI (2)

Nature abides within Love,
Who establishes her boundaries;
Not so with man
Whose fences have been breached
In Freedom's name, and Love's,
On every frontier.

Can humanity afford to ignore,
Charge 'coach & four' through,
The simple truths of Natural Law —
Summed up in Love?

Rather than relearning to Love —
Embracing personal change —
We train to cope with and fight violence.
In other words:
We refuse to recognise the only cure;
Persist in error; disclaim reality.

A: As I intimated a while ago,
Our time has come
And we like lemmings race headlong
Into waves of fun —
Accompanied by song.

Of all our learning
Instinct little knows;
For knowledge
No respect she shows —
Flesh to flesh succumbs.
To rules we have become immune.
(pause)

P: Selfishness respects no law,
Be it natural or Divine.

Ego subsists in self-deception,
Webbing ceaselessly its own truth.

Love lives in Truth.

Canto VII

P: Rules draw for us lines
Where borders are spare
And aid us define
What isn't so clear.

They help us discipline
Both mind and skin;
Said in a nutshell,
Hem chaos in.

A: With modern law and its paid goons
Justice incurs more expense
Than a round-trip to the moon.

Legal faculties themselves
Will be moving their seat soon
From the academy to the saloon.

Rules only serve to verify
What theists rush to vilify:
Our wholly animal nature.
(pause)

P: Our reflective capacity sets us apart
From our primitive origins.
Free will is our prerogative,
To the point of self-destruction.

Self-discipline aligns the mind
In harmony with the eternal soul.
Rules are no more than instruments —
Unimportant in themselves.

A Christian's task is to strive, strive
By grace, toward perfection,
To labour to improve, improve
On imperfection,

Canto VII

Not to lie down and welter in
Mortal frailty
As a well-known species is wont to do
In excrement.

God, in Person,
Journeyed to the earthly paradise
Turned 'vale of tears'
To meet mankind,
Declare, unveil Himself;
Now we are invited to reach one inch,
Raise our hearts to Christ;
Allow Truth's touch thaw out the ice
And grace opportunity to flow again,
Instead of using our humanity
As chicanery to vindicate sin.

To rise to God,
Ties temporal must be loosened, untied, let go . . . .
True whys are humbly acknowledged by
Souls wise to Illusion's lies.

A: Sounds all very fine
Coming from an armchair
Positioned well-behind the front line

But I'm afraid,
Engaging the enemy with: That's not fair!
Will emerge as a joke at the victory parade.

Ownership, Ego's ambassador,
To maximize area of control,
Rubs rules in others' noses which it ignores.

Surely rules amount to tools,
Abetting leaders unruly
Who apply them to organize sheep

Canto VII

Into a hierarchy steep;
Climbing then — leap by leap —
Settle themselves atop the heap.
P: True!
Injured Ego demands redress;
Itself signing dumb or lying low
When it ought to confess.

More the reason
To minimize this cancer's success.

Sin, humanity's defect,
Individual in action
Collective in effect,
Causes all human privation:

Because of one's selfishness,
The whole community suffers.

Conscience, earliest constitution,
That erstwhile sense of sin
Which used to sound an inner din,
Has sadly been retired from public office.

Rules do, nevertheless,
Lend a hand in achieving
Disentanglement from attachments
And assist thereafter maintain distance.

Considering human nature
In the absence of grace,
Attachment tends to enslave:
It binds heart and soul
And drags them to a filthy hold.

In darkness there Soul gropes
And laments at Heart wane cold.

Canto VII

    Responding to prayer,
    Grace lowers some ropes;
    To heave sin-afflicted toward daylight.
A: You're not suggesting surely
    Abandonment of everything;
    Personal and public relationships;
    Intellectual and pleasure pursuits?

P: God first;
    Then everything besides, in perspective!
A: Perspectives change, don't they?
P: Very much so
    While awakening to Truth;
    Less and less though
    As Christ enters one's focal point.
A: While systematically concentrating on belief,
    Can general detachment be achieved?
P: Detachment from the material world,
    Trusting that bit more Divine Succours,
    Favours the ambience
    Vital for spiritual evolvement.

    Fairly utilised, rules liberate —
    Incarcerate poor Chaos;
    Abused, they effectively debilitate,
    Clearing the way for unbridled egos.
A: As to his identity,
    The one upon the cross,
    We are wholly at a loss.
    But, the need for discipline
    Is evidence plenty
    We are the ones 'hemmed in';
    Our liege is Lord Chaos.
P: The order of the earth
    And her occupants therein
    Self-suffice to signature causality.

Canto VII

What basis do you propose
To foot or ground your chaos claim?
A: Chaos has no need of footing.
(pause)
If the order of the earth and so on
Self-suffice to establish cause,
Why umpteen other arguments?
P: To a true believer
Existence itself suffices.
Argument however,
Unnecessitated and uninvited
Of times gatecrashes.

Though believer and polemic flirt,
Neither will the other date:
So this couple relates.

Steadfast prayer fuels faith;
Argument ignites debate:
Thus this quartet equates.

A belief needing defending
Has already lost its case.
A: What about theologians then?
They're not satisfied to stay put.
P: Curiosity, questioning, doubt,
Congenital strengths or weaknesses,
Inhere in self-awareness.

A single argument, if stalwart,
Will support any theory
But several arguments reinforce
And proofs point to certitude.
(pause)
One proof, irrespective of strength,
Triggers sceptics' ongoing dissent.
These doubters in malcontent

Canto VII

Spark off invective at length.

Still, theory and proof,
And libraries of spoof
Cannot compete with Truth.
Truth precedes thought:
Thought rows out in search thereof
And coming to rest, thereon plants its oars.

Many a noble theory was built on sand.
The most well-faced arguments won't protect
A theory against Truth's weathering effect.

On solid sites the works of masters' hands
Ruled proudly a few chapters o'er the lands
But divine are temples that on the waters stand.
A: Each day is filled with accidents
And whims of cosmic origin —
Fate is random: sometimes early; sometimes late.

Adapting to the demands of
Perturbations along their paths,
Some organisms carry on —
Those that learn to adapt —
While those that fail to blend
And please the pace
Are swallowed during their sleep —
For none, to me, is favoured flesh,
Not exempting age-old Earth herself.

And one may argue on:
What was life before it woke?
Where does it go when it has left?
(pause)
Life is nothing outside of here:
I see only mortal footprints

Canto VII

All across Earth's uneven floor;
Of the cosmos contiguous,
No neighbours ease our loneliness.
P: Indeed how true to say,
Life is 'no thing' outside of here.

Before living, life is thought
En route from Truth
To afterlife —
Oneness with the Deity.
Upon conception,
The idea has become
Part of our reality
And waxes toward autonomy.

From within Creator
Issues creation:—
Within Eternity
Commences gestation.

For life mankind is created;
To time a while allocated;
Granted a will unregulated
To deny, admit, accept, reject
Discard, omit, attend, neglect
Truth revealed, or gods elect.

Before Lachesis has done
Either
Illusion has undergone ablation
Or
Its victim, thought strangulation.
A: *(interrupts)*
Death, followed by decay
Synopsises man's destiny!
P: That steers to where it's fated
Contingent on Truth related.

Canto VII

A: So choose it can, but all is dated!
   This being truth, free will's negated.
P: Thus this Faith presents its paradox:
   "Take up your cross and follow Me."

   Dree your weird, submit to Me
   Your will unsteered — I'll lead you free!
A: Can one be free
   After having surrendered
   Unconditionally?
P: Free will surrendered:
   Ego, emasculated;
   Self-slavery, terminated.

   Not capitulation, as appears;
   Rather, joining forces with the Freer.

   For most of us
   Heaven's road-sign points due reverse
   Of our preferred course
   But, however odd God's pointer reads
   Back to Source it surely leads.

   In freedom bounded, choice is clear;
   Where shore's the limit of the lake,
   'Round or up-n-down fish veer.

   Though life beyond the lake seems strange,
   Fish, I'm sure, well imagine
   Funny fishes swimming without.
   (pause)
   If mortal span is one's lake's length,
   Then life goes not 'when it has left'.
A: When riddles near perplex afar,
   Kids build bridges from star to star.
P: Oftentimes today's child's fantasy
   Becomes tomorrow's reality.

Canto VII

(pause)
Your arguments imply,
Correct me if need be,
That everything proceeded from nothingness.

From such a premise one dare move
To corroborate or disprove
What both of us profess:

As matter converges on nothingness
Presumably there'd be observed
A lessening of everything
With variety dissolving . . . .
And so, a place, instant,
Depending on one's 'frame of mind'
Or point of view,
Would present itself as nothing —
Nothingness, void.
Therefore
Some when or where might be described
At which matter materialized.
Can you unriddle how,
Suddenly or otherwise,
Nothing became?
A: 'Became' without a prompt, you mean?
(pause)
All formed simply by slowing down,
Condensing out of force.
P: OK!
But from what source does your force emanate?
A: The old cosmological argument!

The universe, like birth and death,
Like flood and ebb, like peak and pit,
Is a continuum of change:
Cycle within rolling cycle,

Canto VII

Relentlessly alive,
In motion relative.
(pause)
Source smells of finitude.
Why must there be a beginning?
P: Such notion transports us to thought regions
Closed or eternal.
A: Yes!
Eternally changing
From form to form;
Visible to invisible
And vice versa.
P: Isn't your cyclic scheme
At variance with your chaos theme?
A: Our minds have happened to the present state
By virtue of hap association.
Everything known we time relate:
Begin, in being, dead;
This thought, now uttering, has just been said.

How many random thoughts run
Hourly through our heads?
But these are quickly blown
By the gales of chaos
To endless oblivion
Like seeds that never find a soil.

How much effort must be spent
Enforcing daily law and order?
They don't arise voluntarily!
P: That we have happened on this stage
Of thought concatenation
Persuades at least one passing thought to linger
In curious or vacant wonder
If not at the suggestion
Of a certain patronage.

Canto VII

(pause)
Chaos craves for order . . .
A: *(interjects)*
  As a shrew for mastering
  Or the madman, refuge
  From his tormented sea.
P: *(continues)*
  When seen from one vantage spot,
  Matter seems a microscopic chaos;
  Viewed from this celestial dot,
  There appears a macroscopic cosmos.
A: Human society,
  As I've already said,
  Reserves the centre for itself
  Though it is no secret
  We are the latest of the latecomers —
  Forgetful as we tend to be.

  As units of society,
  We exist in a skin of limitations — trepidations —
  Which we project upon our surrounds
  To make the universe reflect ourselves.

  If belief in some higher being were heartfelt,
  Pursuit of wealth wouldn't still outvote all cults.

  God is just another subliminal effort of ours
  To perpetuate our being —
  Another circumscription
  In looking.
P: *(interjects)*
  Do you envisage then
  Any reprieve of this sentence
  Of human limitation?
A: Fantasy, philosophy,
  Fun or religion.

Canto VII

(continues)
All of the tactile universe
Materializes from the invisible
And is absorbed into it again.

Of all Earth's living variety
There was bound to emerge eventually
One species or another that would
Develop more upstairs than elsewhere:—
A kind of cerebral parthenogenesis.

Self-reflection following consciousness;
Either can be accounted for under
"Natural phenomenon."

P: Science observes in nature
Harmonies and symmetries
And tries to harness these
In rules and formulae;

Orthogenesis hasn't gone unnoticed
As it propels mankind
Along with lower plexus
Into higher, more intricate nexus.

From nothingness comes forth
Barren chaos
Order
Life.

A: Order names but one of Chaos's daughters;
Installed at random, each rules and slaughters;
Till some other sibling unexpected
Bursts in and has herself instated.

The universe is night
Dotted throughout with globes of bright.

Canto VIII (1)

A: Church is a building;
    The Bible, a collection of books.
    Sunday's a bad habit
    And the clergy, a bunch of crooks.

    The occult is credible;
    The devil is not.
    God's a myth
    And religion's a pot.

    The spirit's all real;
    That I cannot deny,
    But soul is a something
    I'll believe first at sight or feel
    And am prepared to sit it out
    Till after death reveals
    Or not.
P: Then belief will cease to breathe —
    Which or whether!
A: You sound like someone privy to the absolute!
    A sickness common to all Faiths
    As well as subject of
    Mankind's commonest debate:
    Not to mention the already mentioned
    Breeding ground of conflict and hate.
P: Confirmed belief belongs to knowledge.
    Unconfirmed, it remains
      "The assurance of things hoped for;
      Conviction of things unseen."

    You allow the spirit life 'cause
    You say you can't deny it lives.
    Although you don't vouchsafe the soul
    Your reasons escaped me whole.
A: To accept the soul is to suppose
    Purpose for the pure aligned;

Canto VIII (1)

An ear for the plaintive cry;
An answer to the ill-defined.
P: If not the Soul, what then
Divides the world of creatures
From that of men?
A: The difference, if one insists,
Lies in a different consciousness.
P: Truly, a different consciousness!
Obviously,
Human awareness does exhibit
Some self-reflection,
Which cues Thought to enquire of itself
Why animals, apparently, are solely driven by
"Innate, fixed responses to stimuli,"
Whereas concern for posterity
Or desire for eternity,
Other -ings apart,
Entice the human on.
A: Self-reflection benefits alone ego.
We do love to play 'God',
To set our-puny-selves above it all.
P: You've touched substantial truths there
Since ego beds the roots of sin,
But do you know a better place where
Spirit wandering might come in?
A: Instead of opting for a shed —
A shanty beyond repair —
You'd imagine twould take better care
In choosing a dwelling to house its head.
P: Likewise, the Lord of all
Made début in a stall,
Rode a donkey little
And bade adieu, a criminal.

Why does Ignorance hasten to limit

Canto VIII (1)

What it fails to comprehend?

Or Self-reflection rush to discredit
What Reason cannot defend?
(pause)
Earth receives each one of us;
Our stay, she maintains,
Claiming our remains.
Clearly, she is old
And wherever else we feel savvy —
Inherited; uncovered —
We have been told.

What you call spirit . . . period
Conjoins soul and consciousness,
Sub- through to super-,
In a dialect related to Love.
A: *(thinking to himself)*
Body immersed in greater consciousness . . .
Interesting!
P: *(continuing)*
Square up to, take on, break in ego!
Allow Spirit breathing-space;
Leave rooms, free up a place for it to move . . .
A little patience . . . then
It'll stretch full length its wings and flap
And flap, rising into free flight —

Traversing ceaselessly to and fro
With messages of Love
From mind to soul and back:
Freedom dialogue.
A: If spirit interplays tween mind and soul,
How could plants and animals possess it
In the absence of a mind-soul prerequisite?
P: Both partake of that Spirit,

Canto VIII (1)

Codweller of Another's Mind-Soul,
Similar to the unborn
In its mother's womb.

Every creation, fast or slow,
To some degree, high or low,
Attests to the Universal Spirit —
All life shares in It.
As works of Love's Hands
Created things descend from Love.

A plant's potential to love,
Though much curtailed
Compared to that of an animal,
Enables it, nonetheless, to respond
To being loved and cared for.

Creation and creature's love,
Mimicking their Creator,
Enter into love dialogue

Where love, life reciprocating Love,
Where life, love returning to Source,
Sustain each other; are sustained.

What holds life within it has a spirit
Though it may or may not possess a brain.
A: Sounds a mite like animism.
(pause)
What seeks the restless consciousness of man?
P: What do you reckon?
A: Knowledge, I guess!
P: Knowledge as terminus ad quem
Makes a pathetic surrogate for Truth.

Knowledge may be found and bound,

Canto VIII (1)

Stored and accumulated,
Lost or dissipated,
Reached, but not created.

Though purely an awareness of . . . ,
Being nothing in itself,
Knowing receives the treatment of a have.

Knowledge, one gladly sheds behind
On entering a renewed mind.

Knowledge, skim milk consumed,
Has curdled within: sour lumps in thin;
Learning, a younger culture,
Has yet not settled in — on sin.
(pause)
A: What then?
P: Man seeks a word, a sense, . . .
Something that reconciles, pacifies the world entire;
A solution that satisfies
The equation of the universe.
A: *(retorts)*
Well restless then he will remain
Cause no such word or thing exists!
P: Evidently not in your vocabulary.
A: In the spirit of the insect,
Man seeks the top;
Though in adversity, proves less agile
Than his running mate,
In deceit man does compensate,
Being more adept and nimble.
P: Living is dying
If it's only for life:
Life is destroying
If it's only for self.

Canto VIII (1)

Created body, spirit, soul
In the form of the Creator
We resemble our Originator.

Paralleling somewhat human makings
As they imitate their makers,
We resonate to the Universal Frequency
But backsliding toward ego,
Confer upon ourselves tall credit,
Attribute to ourselves sole merit,
For every morsel we inherit.

A: *(interrupts)*
We certainly do bear lifelong
The trade marks of our makers!

P: *(continues)*
Preferable to aping the Taker,
Would that we might emulate the giver.

As yet this trinity roams confused,
Mutually disoriented,
Explaining thus our restlessness
And inability to function
According to our given potential.

We are earth and ether
Joined and nurtured by Love — the umbilical:
Loving being the zenith expression
Of consciousness — self-reflection.

The extent to which one achieves
Depends on the depth to which one Loves;
Having Loved means having shared one's bread,
Improved, repaired for inequalities left by Greed.

Loving not only lessens the amount
Of selfishness in circulation
But also credits Good's account

Canto VIII (1)

Thus correcting injustice; easing privation.

Improving that doesn't head toward others,
Out of the ego-centred self,
Away from the egocentric family,
Above the ego-ideal society,
Placates illusion; dead-ends itself.

Fostering circumstances conducive to life
Of neighbourhood and next
Encourages peace;
Converts strife.
A: 'Improvements' bring with them
More free time;
Receivers then beast themselves sick
On Boredom's petty crime.

For Majority
Improvements to life's quality to date
Were wrenched brute-like by mobs irate
From stubborn Parasity —
Ensconced in privilege 'by divine right' —
Not conceived of love
Or borne on the wings of a dove.
P: Who would deny
Rape's offspring
The right to life?

Something more remote from God than sin,
Fomenting illness deep within,
Thrusts violence seething through the skin —
Festering pus, erupting.

This thing spurs on,
While its cunning multi-faces grin,
Privilege, and its other duped playthings,

Canto VIII (1)

To violate justice — beget vile things.

Liberties paraded loud'
On wagons slave drawn:
Spoils of victory blood stained —
Seeds of future war, already sown.

Empires* enthral even their overseers.
Vampires demonstrate less inhumanity
In appeasing but their immediate needs,
Leaving at dawn, withdrawing their tyranny.

Gains are never held by stealth or spear
As weapons' strength relies on fear.
If real stability be truly sought,
Not bullied; not opinionated about,
Allow Truth take the steering-wheel;
Lock Liar into the boot, or let walk;
Leave Selfish sulk in the back seat.
A: And this time out
     Everything will be transformed
     Overnight!
P: Man isn't yet at home with
     His recently acquired nous:
     He's still reeling from the shock,
     The aftermath of awakening
     To his quiddity.

The farther he progresses from instinct,
The more global he'll begin to think:
The lower ego will sink,
The more harmonious the trinity,
The more civilised he'll become.

Christ was a person perfectly civilised.

* including modern forms

Canto VIII (1)

To an honest atheist —
Agnostic *id est* —
A Perfect Role Model He remains.
(pause)
Before fair play and justice blind
Brave the side-streets of society's mind,
Violence must be tamed:
Prejudice educated; pride drained;
Justice practised; peace gained;
Truth propagated; honesty sustained.

Fed on righteousness, brute force will yield
A culture to nourish
Its newborn child,
The morrow's new
Humankind.

A: How reliable do you think
That writ-pourri in hallowed ink?

P: The Bible is complete —
Written to the last full-stop —
But the story of man is not.

The Good News remains a-head
In every sense of the Word,
Daily being fulfilled,
Not behind
As defined by Aberration's focus.

Incredible Christ,
Heaped aside on Sceptic's plate,
Sits Inedible.

How humbling to descend
For a Being from a sphere indescribable;
What magnanimity to offer eternity
To beings so wilfully mean!

Canto VIII (1)

A: Well!
   According to your belief,
   Wasn't it He who created them?
P: Not only that . . .
   He doesn't stop there!

   Creator dons humanity:
   "The Word is made flesh,
   And dwells amongst us."

   God becomes flesh and blood,
   Lowers Himself as God alone could,
   So that we may rise
   In paradoxical humility likewise
   To become One
   As did His Son

   And all that's asked of us,
   In all the babbling,
   In all the fuss,
   Is to open our hearts up —
   Partake of the Magnum Opus —
   Like the silent rose . . . unfolding.

Canto VIII (2)

A: You see the human as a synthesis
Of body, mind* and spirit
Where spirit interplays
Between mind and soul.
You omitted mention, though,
Of your concept of the soul.
P: The relationship whole to Whole.
A: Relationship is a pretty extensive term.

P: Relationship is by essence,
A being of a plural kind,
Relating in its quintessence —
Reciprocating proactively or blind.

Relating without communicating
In machine routines abounds
Where souls turn hearts through wall plug-ins
And railroad-minds are laid on purpose grounds.

Communicating initiates growth
Croppings of which reflect the depth of both,
Whereas interaction stimulates
Only the interacting elements.

Acquaintanceship can into friendship grow;
And nourished regularly, develop Love's glow.
In Lukewarm's heart, where flows the status quo,
Love is someone Luke' never gets to know.

Maintenance upkeeps moving parts at new,
Requiring little affection,
But development, mustering its crew,
Exhorts not merely to exertion.

Returning to Eden,
Selecting the tree,
Let's hazard description

* *superconscious — conscious — subconscious*

Canto VIII (2)

Of small trinity:

Root interacts with earth —
Mind and body at work;
Trunk relays leaf to root and back —
Spirit, promoting growth;
Leaves relate to air and light —
Soul, overseeing all.

Soul's a port of entry
To the Eternal Land;
Relating, whole-to-Whole defined,
Describes therein love-trading divine.

Faithfully tracing outlines
Of tripartite humanity
Would require insightings
To the Eternal Mystery:
The Trinity.

A: Relationships have more to do with
Extending one's personality —
Developing one's ego —
Than furthering altruism.
Perhaps your soul synonyms with ego-whole!

P: Because the conscious human mind
Is more familiar to us than
Awareness of any other kind,
And because material and reason
Are with the former so intertwined,
Soul, an alien intrusion,
Becomes a dino* out of season;

Relating, all but inert,
Involves communication of a living sort;
Soul, being no exception,
Responds nowise to dereliction.

* dinosaur

Canto VIII (2)

Denial of the soul
Ignores the most vital member of the whole.
How could true dialogue ever evolve
When Spirit's refused permission to delve?

Dismissing as nought the very thought
Of anything not falling within Reason's pale,
Reduces the mind's monologue
To selective vocab;
Confines thought construction
To the standard prefab.

Three relationships typify us:
Noblest, the living, based on trust;
Commonest, the forced, a question of must;
Worst, selfish: thus far shall I venture just,
Includes the common accurst —
Greed, pride, lust.

Take-take-take drills the ethos of the West —
Ethnocentric breeder of this pest.

Get-get-get, mind-set of both sexes,
Reads the obituary of the intestate.

More! More! More! vociferate
Evaders of moral taxes.

These consuming illnesses thus
Delineate our relationship to Earth and us.
It's as if the human being,
Foremost victim of human excess,
Were not part of the environment.

Preprogrammed to Truth
We each set foot on earth
Regardless of our diminution
Or recognition of the fact.
A: That's a wildish statement — don't you think?

Canto VIII (2)

I'd say, more a flight of fancy than a fact!
P: We are an incarnation of
A universal thought;
An image of an absolute;
A distillation undergoing proof.

All the information of the universe
Is contained in its substance:
A record of the truth —
For the most part undecoded yet.
(pause)
When we contravene this truth,
Consciously or not,
An inner contradiction confronts us:
Frustration erupts,
Unhappiness descends,
Blots out our sun.

Our innermost being hungers,
Our heart longs,
Our mind yearns
For completion.

Substance of the universe,
Epic self-contained,
Divulging you do 'verse
Details of an odyssey ingrained.

Not humble DNA preprogrammings
But a code far subtler in its touching
Infiltrates the entirety of things
Through to the nucleus of being.

Mankind, nonetheless, still enjoys free choice
Wherein Individuality quanders truth
While Companions, of one voice,
Opt enthused for the gossip booth.

Alas!

Canto VIII (2)

Wherever Thought parks its opinion,
If not on truth,
They'll move again.

A: You leave thinkers no peace of mind
And of the residue, not thought inclined,
Paint impressions not overkind.

P: True to character
Prejudicial unevenhandedness
Results less from thought defection
Than thought deflection:
And in the same vein
Truth abuse carries to subsequent rejection.

A: Old Prejudice then has been ousted
From its ancestral seat — ignorance.

P: With ample friends secured
Worry about where to overnight
Won't keep him/her awake.
(pause)
Once one has chosen to reject Truth,
One pines after some substitute
To fill the anonymous vacuum out
And opiate those wanton cravings to boot.

A: Rather a placebo
For ghosts importuning,
Reluctant to go.
(pause)
Does your notion of soul
Allow it possess substance,
Meaning: individuality and form?

P: Soul, native to eternity,
Embryo individual,
Cries out for completeness;
Cries out for a chance at life —
Everlasting bliss.

Its efflorescence hangs on the human will
Which may be spoiled — let run wild
Or disciplined — as must a child.

Canto VIII (2)

A: According to your perception,
   Spirit and soul couldn't possibly be
   Independent entities:
   Without soul, there can be no spirit
   And without the spirit, no relationship.

P: The Whole pervades the universe,
   Transcends eternity
   And continues on . . .

   The human whole
   Composes body-spirit-soul
   Each totally dependent on the Parent Whole.

A: So denying God negates 'one's soul',
   Rendering one incapable of love
   Since the spirit has nowhere to move?

P: Disavowing God negates nothing.
   Opinion just about shifts opinion;
   Reason, struck dumb
   On noticing it has run out of road
   Well within Creation's dominion,
   Reverts to sucking its thumb.

   God, however, exceeds logic
   And contradictions, which stir up stress
   In the waters of human weakness,
   So, has no use for dialectic.

   God's radiance eclipses knowledge —
   Everything knowable.
   Reason and logic could travel forever
   But approach Him one inch, neither would — never
   Since nothing created can of itself reach Him.

   God, Author Supreme, Loves:
   That's what He is; that's what He does.
   This Being may be contacted
   By dialling from the heart.

Canto VIII (2)

A: How can one know anything about
   The soil and climate of a land
   Far, far across the sea
   When one hasn't got the remotest clue
   As to whether there is or isn't terra firma there?

P: We have the testimony of those who
   Bore witness to what eludes both me and you.

   And, what saints of ages lived and left behind
   Lingers as silent testament in the mind,
   Bringing to light, putting to flight
   Time upon time again
   Lies of feeble-minded self-deception.

   Terra incognita sparks off thought
   Which lures science from its burrow out —
   From obscurity into sight.

   The world is wider than this village;
   Broader than this nation; this wee continent;
   This tiny planet; this infinitesimal system:

   Life is greater than this moment;
   The human span; an age.

   But Columbus gets continually told,
   Ridiculed by the bold:
   The edge of the Earth is the end
   And no thinking mind would dare send
   Its thoughts round an imaginary bend.
   (pause)

A: When reason is reduced in price
   And imagination declared hard currency,
   Superstition goes on a shopping spree.

P: Where reason becomes overvalued
   And faith, underfed,
   The balance of progress slumps into red.

Canto IX (1)

A: Empiricism is the road to knowledge.
P: How might one reach that conclusion?
A: All the useful knowledge we have to date
   Came a posteriori, not through revelation —
   And most certainly not through faith!

P: When Trial and Error discovered that
   Square pegs fitted square holes best,
   They settled down to shape thought's rest
   So all the world would neatly fit.

   Because logic cannot be fitted to faith
   Any more than reason can to revelation,
   There's more reason to mourn logic's limitations
   Than to celebrate the death of Faith and Revelation.

   Logic's not the only route to knowing:
   There's another, via faith.
   Forsaking the comfort of reasoning,
   Watching it sink below,
   One meets the strangeness of wisdom
   Egressing from one's being's core.
A: One can't just disregard reason:
   It has given us all we've got!
P: Undoubtedly, it has . . .
   'Given us all we've got!'
   One need but glance at
   The current state of Earth.
   (pause)
   Neither ought one pour slight on faith
   Simply 'cause one knows it not.

   When Reason reaches the hill-top,
   There it has to stop
   But Faith carries on above the drop.
   Reason hugs the curves of Earth,

Canto IX (1)

While Faith prefers to fly.

Faith arrives at knowing,
Having bypassed knowledge.

That one lacks faith proves not
That God is not;
Nor does it discredit Christ.
(pause)
Dearth of faith shows only
One's surplus of cowardice
When challenged by humility.
(pause)
Sole reliance on human reason
Characterises tunnel vision
Or the edges of one's capacity to think —
Hall-mark of rationalism's pride.

Weak faith's an inkling of reality;
Strong faith, death before one dies.

Sincere and earnest atheism is
A most dangerous state to live in
For in the event of stumbling on one's crutches,
Rest assured, one will encounter the Real Thing.

Agnosticism, at worst bedridden
At best, a wheelchair case
Courts not a miracle
Lest it lead to apostasy.

Wishy-Washy's the cosiest nest on Earth:
Wobbling or wavering connotes no risk.
A: Faith!
"Unquestioning belief,
Requiring neither proof nor evidence . . ."

Canto IX (1)

How brilliantly convenient!

P: 'Unquestioning belief' takes as much a part as reason,
If not more, in the everyday:
Preparing to take a seat
Doesn't necessitate close scrutiny
To reassure oneself
The chair can bear the advent weight;

Riding daily ten stories up or down,
One takes the lift on faith . . .

A: *(interjects)*
You mean, for granted!

P: *(continues)*
While contemplating between floors
Weaker probabilities than
Mechanical or power malfunction.

A: Faith has two dwelling-places:
The first stands on experience;
The second floats on air.

P: Substantiated belief has left faith;
Has lodged on fact.

If one truly believes in something,
Has faith that is,
One doesn't look for back-up data.

A: What does one do?

P: Lives according to that belief!
(pause)

A: Don't faiths, to begin with,
Rely on certain minima of facts?
Something has to start the ball rolling!

P: *(thinking)*
Revealing.

P: *(replying)*
Belief in Eternity
Wells from the inner human.

Canto IX (1)

Person by person we repress and purge
Or release its gentle, inexorable surge.
Conviction in a particular confession
Originates from personae plus matching acts.

True faith inspires charity — love;
All 'faith' besides incites calumnies — lies.

By experiencing the gift of faith,
A person responds to the invitation
To enter into the Eternal's life.

Rejecting faith,
Free Will chooses non-participation
In non-justifiable belief . . .

Ignoring by choice
Or unfit to see maybe
Therein the contradiction.
(pause)
(digression)
Wishy-Washies,
Grouped together in lukewarmness,
Turn borderline-believers off;
Switch critics on.

These middle-of-the-roaders assert,
In their inspired insight into the eternal depths,
Faith alone secures salvation:—
Meaning therewith
Acquiescence to some hazy deity —
Brainchild of the invertebrate —
Provides ample premium cover
Should one need to claim on
The uncertain afterlife.

Never daring to scratch the surface self —

Canto IX (1)

Polished by habitude, social track —
They content themselves with the cosmetic
Sooner than face the truth side of the mask
And ask:
Could faith received suggest some giving back?

'Belief in an Eternal Being passes muster!'
They hold forth, as if more were inordinate.

Total faith places all at His feet
Alike in joy as in defeat.
Anything less constitutes reserved belief
And brings doubt lying into relief.
(end of digression)

A: Looks like almost a whole society
Of backsliders has stood you up.
(pause)
Well, since few peruse
Let alone practise
Any kind of living philosophy
Beyond an echo of Majority's,
Theism, your kind, amounts to
Foul-weather friendship
To quote cliché.

P: Atheism relies no less on faith
Than does theism: both are beliefs.
Your last remarks bespeak
No more than human dishonesty.
In the case Deus versus Chance
Atheism presents deficiency of evidence
As evidence of non-existence.
With such lightweight reasoning
It ought not be unreasonable
To alight 'logically' on rain-cloud.

A: To prove that 'God' exists
Establishes, in fact, the opposite:

Canto IX (1)

A proof, containing as it does
Both root and stem,
Must be superior in strength
To that which it supports.

P: *(jesting)*
    Superior!
    Logic seems to sanction hierarchy.
    (pause)
    A proof may be treated
    As a ladder used to grasp
    Desired but distant fruit.

    Stems do look pretty bleak
    Not having managed to produce
    Those blossoms the roots seek.

    Creation, a flower,
    Feeds off Eternal Juice
    Through Stem invisible
    From Root unreachable.

A: Language has its limitations:
    It doesn't always quite measure up to thought.

    Let's apply a rephrasing:
    To achieve success,
    A proof besieging
    Must wholly encompass.

P: If, as sceptics propose,
    Absence of evidence
    Offers reason to suppose
    No Eternal presence,
    How do they diagnose
    Evidence of absence?

A: Show me some evidence!

P: If existence itself doesn't suffice,
    The total of fingerprints
    That sums up the universe

Canto IX (1)

Couldn't convince.
(pause)
Do you cease being
On turning the corner,
When my thoughts of you have stopped?

Does the topic disappear
Subsequent to its having been dropped?

At touch of Time's bounds, Thought halted abrupt';
Thinking it over, Thought overstepped.
(long pause)
When one can prove everything,
Then one has replaced God:—
Precisely what scientific man attempts.
Incidentally,
Could you try proving
That you actually exist?

A: Something self-evident
Serves as its own proof.
No further witness need be called.

P: Then, accordingly
Something self-evident would be
Superior to itself?

A: Yea!
Holistically speaking.

P: So an hypothetical absolute,
Assuming such to be the roof,
Would have no proof?
(pause)

A: Were such a proof at hand,
Twould silence all dispute
Since no-one need refute
Evidence which gainsaid its own stand.
(pause)
That leads us back to no-man's-land.

Canto IX (1)

P: Upon raising of the blinds,
   Even Thomas conceded the New Day.
   (pause)
   Could not an Absolute Mind,
   Using logic of finer mesh,
   Furnish affirmation of Itself?
A: If It were,
   I have no doubt It would.
P: One Lamb appears inadequate
   To satiate the ever hungry wolf.

   Scribe and Pharisee still insist
   That Perfect conform on 'request'
   To Imperfect's contradictory test
   But Mr Perfect outclevers, while fast asleep,
   Together the forum of sophists.

   Were God to reappear in Person,
   Sceptics would again demand miracles;
   Were such once more forthcoming,
   Explanation would heel explanation
   As happened then
   And has since been happening.

   God,
   The greatest paradox
   That Thought has ever trod on:
   Too obvious to perceive;
   Too simple to accept;
   Is the point of vacuum where
   Reason buckles beneath faith.